WOMEN WHO DARE

Eleanor Roosevelt

BY
ANJELINA MICHELLE KEATING

Pomegranate
SAN FRANCISCO

LIBRARY OF CONGRESS
WASHINGTON, DC

Published by Pomegranate Communications, Inc.
Box 808022, Petaluma CA 94975
800 227 1428; www.pomegranate.com

Pomegranate Europe Ltd.
Unit 1, Heathcote Business Centre, Hurlbutt Road
Warwick, Warwickshire CV34 6TD, UK
[+44] 0 1926 430111; sales@pomeurope.co.uk

Amy Pastan, Series Editor

In association with the Library of Congress, Pomegranate publishes other books in the Women Who Dare® series, as well as calendars, books of postcards, posters, and Knowledge Cards® featuring daring women. Please contact the publisher for more information.

Library of Congress Cataloging-in-Publication Data

Keating, Anjelina Michelle.
     Eleanor Roosevelt / by Anjelina Michelle Keating.
        p. cm. — (Women who dare)
     Includes bibliographical references.
     ISBN 0-7649-3543-7
     1. Roosevelt, Eleanor, 1884–1962. 2. Roosevelt, Eleanor, 1884–1962—Pictorial works. 3. Presidents' spouses—United States—Biography. 4. Presidents' spouses—United States—Pictorial works. I. Library of Congress. II. Title. III. Women who dare (Petaluma, Calif.)

E807.1.R48K43 2006
973.917092—dc22
[B]

                                                                                              2005049544

Pomegranate Catalog No. A109
Designed by Harrah Lord, Yellow House Studio, Rockport ME
Printed in Korea

15 14 13 12 11 10 09 08 07 06   10 9 8 7 6 5 4 3 2 1

FRONT COVER: Eleanor at the 1940 Democratic National Convention. AP/WORLDWIDE
BACK COVER: Eleanor at her husband's first inauguration, 1933. LC-USZ62-112743

PREFACE

FOR TWO HUNDRED YEARS, the Library of Congress, the oldest national cultural institution in the United States, has been gathering materials necessary to tell the stories of women in America. The last third of the twentieth century witnessed a great surge of popular and scholarly interest in women's studies and women's history that has led to an outpouring of works in many formats. Drawing on women's history resources in the collections of the Library of Congress, the Women Who Dare book series is designed to provide readers with an entertaining introduction to the life of a notable American woman or a significant topic in women's history.

From its beginnings in 1800 as a legislative library, the Library of Congress has grown into a national library that houses both a universal collection of knowledge and the mint record of American creativity. Congress' decision to purchase Thomas Jefferson's personal library to replace the books and maps burned during the British occupation in 1814 set the Congressional Library on the path of collecting with the breadth of Jefferson's interests. Not just American imprints were to be acquired, but foreign-language materials as well, and Jefferson's library already included works by American and European women.

The Library of Congress has some 121 million items, largely housed in closed stacks in three buildings on Capitol Hill that contain twenty public reading rooms. The incredible, wide-ranging collections include books, maps, prints, newspapers, broadsides, diaries, letters, posters, musical scores, photographs, audio and video recordings, and documents available only in digital formats. The Library serves first-time users and the most experienced researchers alike.

I hope that you, the reader, will seek and find in the pages of this book information that will further your understanding of women's history. In addition, I hope you will continue to explore the topic of this book in a library near you, in person at the Library of Congress, or by visiting the Library on the World Wide Web at http://www.loc.gov. Happy reading!

—JAMES H. BILLINGTON, The Librarian of Congress

■ *Portrait of Eleanor Roosevelt, c. 1945.* LC-USZ62-107008

Perhaps the most important thing that has come out of my life is the discovery that if you prepare yourself at every point as well as you can, with whatever means you may have, however meager they may seem, you will be able to grasp opportunity for broader experience when it appears. . . . Life was meant to be lived, and curiosity must be kept alive. One must never, for whatever reason, turn his back on life.

—Eleanor Roosevelt, Hyde Park, December 1960

The name *Eleanor Roosevelt* most likely conjures images of a bold, progressive, and accomplished woman well known for her dedication to improving the lives of the disadvantaged, her intense focus on social reform, and her unshakable belief in the indelible rights of every human being. She was also, however, a woman who struggled throughout her life with feelings of failure, abandonment, and low self-worth, a woman who questioned her ability to be a good mother, a woman susceptible to periods of dark depression. Despite her troubles, Eleanor Roosevelt had a passionate desire to contribute to her world, wanting only, as she said, "the opportunity for doing something useful, for in no other way, I am convinced, can true happiness be attained."

In her quest for usefulness, Eleanor worked closely with many activist organizations of her time and participated in key events to promote equality

■ *Eleanor with civil rights activists Rosa Parks (left) and Autherine Lucy (right), New York City, 1956.* LC-USZ62-111444

and fairness for women, members of minority groups, and workers. Having forged a potent political partnership with her husband, President Franklin Delano Roosevelt, she provided support and guidance for her nation during the tumultuous 1930s and 1940s, the trying times of the Great Depression and World War II. Later in life, after becoming the first woman appointed to

■ *Eleanor admires a copy of the Universal Declaration of Human Rights, translated into Spanish, 1949. The effort to produce the United Nations document had consumed several years of her life.* FDR LIBRARY

■ *Eager to have her views heard, Eleanor capitalized on every possible medium, using interviews, lectures, print, radio, and even the newly invented television. In 1950, she appeared on NBC to weigh in on controversy regarding the hydrogen bomb.* LC-USZ62-92100

the US delegation to the United Nations, she oversaw the drafting of the United Nations' Universal Declaration of Human Rights.

Eleanor challenged the traditional roles of Victorian femininity she had grown up with, as well as those associated with the position of First Lady. Refusing to be relegated to the role of hostess, she held her own press conferences, delivered lectures, and traveled the world, reporting back to the polio-stricken president about the conditions she encountered.

■ *En route to the White House, Eleanor, who also became known to family, friends, and the public as ER, relaxes with her visitor, Britain's Queen Elizabeth, 1939.*

LC-USZ62-111580

Although deeply committed to her beliefs, she remained open-minded and relished discussion and debate, revising and fine-tuning her viewpoints year by year. Never defeated by feelings of failure stemming from a difficult youth, she continually searched for ways to reach out to the people around her, to alleviate suffering, to effect change—efforts that earned her the nickname "First Lady of the World."

■ *In this photograph, c. 1892, Eleanor poses with her father, Elliott Roosevelt, and her younger brothers, Gracie Hall (b. 1891) and Elliott Jr. (b. 1889). Shortly after this, she suffered the loss of her beloved father, her brother Elliott Jr., and her mother. "Hall" passed away in 1941 after a lifelong struggle with alcoholism.* FDR LIBRARY

A Painful Youth

ELEANOR'S BEGINNINGS seemed promising; she was born into a high-society family that enjoyed power, wealth, and respect. However, during her childhood and as a young woman, she was often told that she was not good enough, a message that left her lonely and isolated and scarred her psyche for years to come. Emerging from childhood, she was a shy, timid young woman haunted by low self-esteem, one who consistently deferred to others and who felt uncomfortable in social settings, detested looking foolish, and often avoided trying new things. It would take more than thirty years for an independent, confident Eleanor to emerge.

Born October 11, 1884, Anna Eleanor Roosevelt was the eldest child of Anna Hall (Roosevelt), a New York society belle, and Elliott Roosevelt, member of the influential Oyster Bay Roosevelt branch and younger brother of Theodore Roosevelt, who would become president in 1901. Eleanor would be orphaned by her tenth birthday, but before then, both parents would make lasting impressions on her. Her mother was, in Eleanor's words, "one of the most beautiful women I have ever seen," but uncomfortable with Eleanor's plain looks, she was quite critical of her young daughter. Eleanor recalled:

> . . . still I can remember standing in the door, often with my finger in my mouth, and I can see the look in her eyes and hear the tone of her voice as she said, "Come in, Granny." If a visitor was there she might turn and say, "She is such a funny child, so old-fashioned that we always call her 'Granny.'" I wanted to sink through the floor in shame.

■ *Franklin and Eleanor enjoy Campobello, an island off the coast of Maine, c. 1920. As a youth, FDR often summered there, a tradition he continued with his own family. In 1921, he was stricken with polio while at Campobello.*

FDR LIBRARY

The sense of shame her mother imparted left Eleanor, even before Anna's death in 1892, with a keen sense of abandonment; her unmet need for love and acceptance developed into a deep longing that would follow her through life. Her father was more successful at connecting warmly with his daughter, and Eleanor adored Elliott, calling him "the love of my life." However, in many ways he was not a capable father. Prone to depression and an alcoholic, Elliott showed early signs of self-destructiveness; his marriage was troubled and ultimately doomed, and he was often absent from young Eleanor's life. Eleanor hoped that she and her father would someday "have a life of our own together," but instead she was sent to live with her maternal grandmother, Mary Ludlow Hall. There, after the death of both her mother and a younger brother from diphtheria, she learned of her father's death as well. He died in 1894 from a fall he suffered after drinking heavily. "I simply refused to believe it," she said, but it was true. Eleanor was not yet ten, but her childhood was, in a sense, over.

When she was fifteen, Eleanor left the United States for England to attend the esteemed Allenswood Academy. Under the tutelage of headmistress Marie Souvestre, she blossomed. A solemn, serious girl who felt "lost and very lonely" when she arrived at Allenswood, Eleanor began to discover and cultivate strengths: leadership, deep compassion and caring for others, responsibility, and a surprising popularity—accompanied by an ability to influence. Souvestre saw curiosity, intelligence, and potential behind her student's shy exterior, and she prodded Eleanor to come out of her shell. In particular, she nudged her student toward social work, which Eleanor eagerly continued on her return to New York. There she joined the

Junior League and the National Consumers' League, investigating working conditions in factories and interacting with children from impoverished families.

Calling the Allenswood experience "the happiest years of my life," Eleanor would gladly have gone on to college, but her family saw no value in educating women. Instead, they prepared her for an introduction to society in hopes that she would find a suitable husband. She found one in a distantly removed cousin, the charming, flirtatious, and commanding Franklin Delano Roosevelt, a member of the influential and respected Hyde Park Roosevelt branch. Although his overbearing mother, Sara Delano Roosevelt, opposed the match, Eleanor and Franklin were married in 1905 (her uncle, President Theodore Roosevelt, escorted her down the aisle). Between 1906 and 1916, they had six children together; five survived into adulthood.

Eleanor was insecure about her ability to be a capable, nurturing parent, but was enthusiastic about fulfilling her new roles of wife, mother, and daughter-in-law. Her uncertainties, however, were intensified by her mother-in-law, who adored her son and sought to control every aspect of the new couple's lives, even giving them a New York City home next to her own with connecting interior doors. Sara interfered as Eleanor raised her children, acting as if they were her own and telling them, "Your mother only bore you." Having been deprived of a loving family life as a child and

■ *The Roosevelt family, Washington, DC, 1919. One of Eleanor's six children died in infancy; pictured here are Anna Eleanor (b. 1906), James (b. 1907), Elliott (b. 1910), Franklin Jr. (b. 1914), and John (b. 1916).* FDR LIBRARY

desperate for the approval and love of her husband and mother-in-law, Eleanor suffered through such abuse. Her desperation led to passive, deferential behavior. Later, she remarked, "I was beginning to be an entirely dependent person . . . someone always had to decide everything for me," and described herself early in her marriage as "a weak character."

Eleanor dutifully followed as Franklin pursued his interest in politics—he won a term in the New York State Senate in 1910 and moved on to Washington, DC, to serve as assistant secretary of the navy in 1913—but she remained politically ignorant, believing that politics held no place for women. Even as the women's suffrage movement intensified around her, she showed little interest. Incredibly, Eleanor, who later worked vigorously for women's rights, initially opposed the suffrage movement, unable to reconcile its message with the values instilled during her upbringing. When she finally changed her stance, initially it was only because her husband supported suffrage:

> I took it for granted that men were superior creatures and knew more about politics than women did, and while I realized that if my husband was a suffragist I probably must be, too, I cannot claim to have been a feminist in those early days.

Women's societal roles were evolving, though, as the pressures of World War I made women's increased involvement vital. Seeds of activism sprouted in Eleanor as she worked diligently for the Red Cross in Washington, DC. Her family had always stressed the importance of

■ *The Roosevelts' Hyde Park home in New York, 1933. Nicknamed the "summer White House," FDR's family estate, presided over by Sara Delano Roosevelt, was not a place where Eleanor felt comfortable. She remarked, "For over 40 years, I was only a visitor there."*
LC-USZ62-128439

benevolence and charity, so this was not a particularly extraordinary role for her. However, it seems to have been the first step on Eleanor's path toward a more active and fulfilling life, for in many ways the early years of her marriage were just as unhappy as her childhood had been.

■ *Portrait of the United States' newest First Lady, Eleanor Roosevelt, 1933.* LC-USZC4-5768

AN INDEPENDENT LIFE

HISTORIANS HAVE DEBATED what sparked Eleanor's transformation from a submissive, passive woman into a commanding political force, an advocate for social causes who would not hesitate to challenge anyone. Perhaps her Red Cross activities during World War I whetted her appetite for more satisfying work. After her last child was born, in 1916, she may have experienced greater freedom as she was no longer confined so often to her home. Her discovery in 1918 of her husband's affair with her social secretary, Lucy Mercer—an event that deeply hurt Eleanor, shattering her sense of family and compelling her to offer Franklin a divorce—may also have spurred her to carve out a more independent life. Although the Roosevelts elected not to separate, their marriage underwent great change, eventually resembling a business partnership more than an intimate relationship, and Eleanor began forming many rewarding friendships outside her marriage. Franklin's bout with polio in 1921, which left his legs paralyzed, also may have convinced her of the necessity for a more politically powerful role. Fully supporting Franklin's involvement in politics, she encouraged him to continue his career even after polio struck. In the process, she at last won a major battle with Sara Delano, who wanted him to give up politics and enjoy a quiet country life.

Whatever the reason, Eleanor's days of deference were over, and in the 1920s she began to develop into a confident, independent person. She approached life with a gusto and self-assuredness she had not previously enjoyed, started volunteer work in earnest, and quickly became involved with a multitude of activist groups: the League of Women Voters, the Women's Trade Union League, and the Women's Division of the New

■ *Poster promoting the Red Cross during World War I. The Red Cross and the Navy–Marine Corps Relief Society were among the first organizations with which Eleanor worked closely; her involvement awakened a new sense of purpose in her life.*
LC-USZC4-7763

York State Democratic Committee. For the first time in her life, she was surrounded by strong female role models: Elizabeth Read and Esther Lape of the League of Women Voters; Caroline O'Day, who was involved with the Women's Division; and staunch Democrats Marion Dickerman and Nancy Cook, with whom Eleanor would form a lasting partnership. Along with Dickerman and Cook, Eleanor formed Val-Kill Industries at Val-Kill, the New York home Franklin had built for her, creating a furniture factory to provide jobs for underprivileged youth. They also owned and operated the Todhunter School in New York City, where Eleanor taught history, literature, and current events. She continued teaching even after Franklin was elected governor of New York in 1928, which forced her to commute from Albany: "It gave me an opportunity for regular work," she said, "which I was anxious to have."

■ *Franklin, then governor of New York, and Eleanor visit President Herbert Hoover at the White House, 1932. Eleanor was no stranger to the presidential residence: she had often visited her father's older brother Theodore, well known as "Teddy," when he occupied it from 1901 to 1909.*

LC-USZ62-91121

Far from living in the shadow of her increasingly successful husband, Eleanor was developing a public face of her own. Intensely involved in the Democratic Party's women's divisions on both the state and national levels, she assisted in the Democratic national campaign for the presidency in 1928, the same year that Franklin became governor of New York. She emerged as an advocate for women's issues, unwavering in her resolve to ensure that the party appealed to women and in her efforts to mobilize them to exercise their new right to vote. "It is always disagreeable to take stands," she remarked. "It is always easier to compromise, always easier to let things go. To many women, and I am one of

■ *New York governor Franklin Delano Roosevelt is surrounded by a crowd while campaigning for the presidency, Hyde Park, New York, 1932.* LC-USZ62-117439

them, it is extremely difficult to care about anything enough to cause disagreement or unpleasant feelings, but I have come to the conclusion that this must be done for a time until we can prove our strength and demand respect for our wishes."

Throughout the 1920s and into the 1930s, Eleanor became increasingly skilled in public speaking, writing, and editing, and, most important, developed a political savvy that would serve her well in 1933, when she would occupy her most demanding public position yet—First Lady of the United States of America.

■ *Eleanor and her husband in New York City, 1934, with their eldest son, James, James' first wife, and FDR's mother, Sara Delano Roosevelt.*
FDR LIBRARY

■ *Eleanor with FDR, Caroline O'Day (in car), and Fiorello LaGuardia, 1938. O'Day, a New York congresswoman, met Eleanor while both were active in the Women's Division of the State Democratic Committee. In 1941, Eleanor worked closely with LaGuardia when he headed the Office of Civilian Defense.*
LC-USZ62-128044

ELEANOR AS FIRST LADY

AS FRANKLIN endured his first campaign for the presidency, Eleanor grew increasingly apprehensive. She questioned whether she would be able to maintain her independent life in Washington, DC, and remarked to her new friend Lorena Hickok, an Associated Press reporter assigned to cover Eleanor during the campaign, "I never wanted to be a President's wife, and don't want it now." However, encouraged by both Hickok and Louis Howe—one of Franklin's political advisors, whom she had met during FDR's unsuccessful bid for the vice presidency in 1920 and who became her political mentor—Eleanor quickly realized that her new position would afford her ample opportunity to accomplish social reform in the United States. Despite her worries and her distaste for the demands of living in the White House and in the public eye, Eleanor Roosevelt became one of the most effective and extraordinary First Ladies in history.

Eleanor had no desire to be restricted to the household duties of a Washington wife, as she had been when Franklin was assistant secretary of the navy in 1913. Therefore, when FDR was elected president, she asked whether she could assist him with his mail or in some other administrative capacity. He told her he already had a capable assistant—Marguerite "Missy" LeHand, who had been at his side since 1920—and needed no other. Obviously, it would be up to Eleanor to find her own meaningful work.

Eleanor came to the White House at a particularly opportune time to carry out the social work she found so fulfilling, for when Franklin took office in 1933, the United States was in the grip of a debilitating depression,

■ *FDR delivers his first inaugural speech at the US Capitol, March 4, 1933.*
LC-USZ62-18168

which would be further aggravated by the impending dust bowl, a massive land erosion calamity that befell some southwestern states. The carefree prosperity of the 1920s was over, but Eleanor was willing to work harder than ever. As First Lady, she answered thousands of letters written to her, forwarding specific ones to those in the administration who could best help the writer. She strove to link Franklin's administration to the people he

■ *Election Day 1940: On their way to vote, Franklin and Eleanor ride together in Hyde Park. "He might have been happier with a wife who was completely uncritical," she would later say. "That I was never able to be, and he had to find it in other people."*
LC-USZ62-1115844

served. By the time FDR assumed office, the couple had begun to perfect their political partnership, and throughout his twelve years as president, Eleanor would bring various progressive causes to his attention and use her unique position to encourage change. She described their relationship this way: "I'm the agitator; he's the politician."

Early on, Eleanor realized that to be a voice for those in need, she must be heard. In 1933, she began holding her own press conferences, something no First Lady had ever done. Further, she limited the gatherings to female reporters—a move that triggered additional hiring of women by newspapers. Not stopping there, Eleanor addressed the nation in radio programs, on the lecture circuit—becoming an extremely popular public speaker—and in a nationally syndicated newspaper column titled "My Day," affording her views greater visibility than enjoyed by any of her predecessors. Eleanor's "My Day" columns quickly evolved into political commentaries addressing a broad spectrum of subjects, from race riots and desegregation to equality for women and women's role in World War II.

Eleanor did not occupy an official role in assisting Franklin with his New Deal legislation, which provided economic stability to the suffering nation in the form of increased government influence, aid, and programs offering employment, but she almost certainly held considerable influence; journalist Raymond Clapper wrote that she had "almost the importance of a cabinet minister without portfolio." She persuaded Franklin to appoint women to his administration, and she could be expected to critique him just as easily as she might offer support. Admired by many, she also garnered her share of criticism, often from those who thought she should play a more subdued role as First Lady. Malvina Thompson, Eleanor's longtime secretary and friend, defended her, saying, "People who criticize her simply don't know what they're talking about. They don't understand the meaning of her activities. Or they just unconsciously resent her being so different from other Presidents' wives." Having made it clear from the beginning that she intended to be a very different kind of president's wife,

■ *Poster for the Civilian Conservation Corps, an early New Deal effort to provide work opportunities for youth, c. 1941.*
LC-USZC4-1588

■ *Poster, c. 1937, promoting the National Youth Administration, an organization that provided employment and education for young men and women.*
LC-USZC2-5552

■ *Des Moines, Iowa, 1936: Eleanor visits a Works Progress Administration site. The WPA helped US citizens stalled by the Great Depression to return to work.* FDR LIBRARY

Eleanor took the sometimes biting criticism in stride, writing, "Every woman in public life needs to develop skin as tough as rhinoceros hide."

Dismayed by the poverty she encountered while touring the United States early in her tenure as First Lady, Eleanor attempted to better the lives of the distressed and impoverished, and she was involved in many of the famed Works Progress Administration's programs of FDR's New Deal. She took a leading role in the Arthurdale project, a progressive but unsuccessful settlement program intended to create jobs in West Virginia. Equally concerned about the country's youth, in part because she linked the success of fascism abroad to the malaise of younger citizens, she supported young people's political endeavors, encouraging liberal reform organizations such as the American Student Union and the American Youth Congress. She also worked tirelessly to provide unemployed citizens with meaningful work, becoming closely involved in the creation of the National Youth Administration. There, she was instrumental in getting civil rights activist Mary McLeod Bethune appointed to an advisory position from which she could promote the concerns of both minorities and women.

Eleanor's friendship with Bethune and many other civil rights activists was notable given that she, like many in the United States, had been raised in an atmosphere of racial intolerance—even on her entry into the White House, she still referred to African Americans as "darkies." However, she quickly became aware of the persistent racism plaguing the nation and transformed herself into an outspoken advocate for civil rights, demonstrating once again her ability to transcend her ingrained social views.

During her husband's first term in office, Eleanor worked with Walter White on behalf of the National Association for the Advancement of Colored People, bringing to Franklin's attention the need for anti-lynching legislation. Although she did not succeed in getting this legislation passed, largely because Franklin was dependent on the support of southern senators for his New Deal legislation, she continued to draw attention to racial inequalities. On arriving at the Southern Conference for Human Welfare in Alabama in 1939, Eleanor found that seating was segregated; in protest,

■ *Mary McLeod Bethune and Eleanor Roosevelt at a National Youth Administration meeting, between 1935 and 1943. Bethune, a civil rights activist and educator, owed her NYA advisory position to Eleanor's intervention.* LC-USZ62-117627

■ *Eleanor presents Marian Anderson with the NAACP's Spingarn Medal, 1939. The medal is awarded annually to an exceptional black American.* LC-USZ62-116730

she set up her own folding chair in the separating aisle and refused to budge. That same year, she resigned her membership with the Daughters of the American Revolution when the organization barred African American contralto Marian Anderson from singing at its concert hall. In her "My Day" column, she wrote, "To remain a member implies approval of that action, and therefore I am resigning." Eleanor's support helped

■ *In 1945, Eleanor joined the NAACP's board of directors. In this 1947 photograph, she and fellow board member James McClendon are surrounded by NAACP officers Walter White, Roy Wilkins, and Thurgood Marshall.* LC-USZ62-84463

■ *New York City, 1942: Eleanor attends an event honoring African American achievement and visits with troops serving their country in World War II.* LC-USZ62-133298

Anderson sing in Washington after all, at a well-attended outdoor concert at the Lincoln Memorial. By 1945, Eleanor had joined the NAACP's board of directors. White House housekeeper Henrietta Nesbitt remarked, "With Mrs. Roosevelt it was intellect that mattered. I don't believe she noticed a person's color any more than she did their dress."

Regarding war, Eleanor held pacifistic views, but these views were

■ *Raised among stifling anti-Semitic and racist sentiments, Eleanor did much to overcome her upbringing and embrace the world's diversity. Here, c. 1940, she rubs noses with a New Zealand Maori woman in a traditional Maori greeting.* LC-USZ62-64437

challenged as she watched fascism and ultranationalism spread across the world, and she committed herself wholeheartedly to the United States' involvement in World War II. Her aversion to tyranny overthrew her disgust for war, although she remained acutely aware of war's human cost. During World War II, she carried a poem-prayer with her that posed a question she worked incessantly to answer:

Lest I continue
My complacent way,
Help me to remember that somewhere
Somehow out there
A man died for me today.
As long as there be war,
I then must
Ask and answer
Am I worth dying for?

Issues long near her heart were visible in Eleanor's wartime work as she fought racial discrimination in the armed forces; worked to help refugees, particularly children, find safe harbor in the United States; and recommended that women be allowed a greater role in the war. "Life in the armed services is hard and uncomfortable," she stated, "but I think women can stand up under that type of living just as well as men."

In 1941, Eleanor took an official position within the government—becoming the first president's wife to do so. Appointed assistant director of the Office of Civilian Defense, she worked closely with its director, New York City mayor Fiorello LaGuardia. Eleanor was well qualified for the position, but it brought her some of the most intense criticism of her life—her official role made her an ideal target for opponents of the president and his New Deal policies—and she resigned after a few months. Although she gave up a defined public role in FDR's administration, Eleanor remained vocal and active during World War II. She visited troops at home and abroad to boost morale and to report on conditions to Franklin, brushing

■ *Eleanor greets female soldiers at Sampson Air Force Base, Geneva, New York, c. 1943.*
FDR LIBRARY

aside the notion of personal danger. In 1943, she toured Australia and the South Pacific, where she impressed Admiral William Halsey Jr., who had been anticipating her arrival with dread. He wrote later: "When I say that she inspected those hospitals, I don't mean that she shook hands with the chief medical officer, glanced into a sun parlor, and left. I mean that she went into every ward, stopped at every bed, and spoke to every patient: What was his name? How did he feel? Was there anything he needed?

■ *In addition to meeting with notables on her international inspection tours, Eleanor called on American troops stationed abroad. Here, she samples chow at an army kitchen on Galápagos Island in the South Pacific, 1944.*
FDR LIBRARY

■ *Eleanor speaks with a female machinist in Great Britain, 1942. During the war, women took on increasingly important roles on the home front.* LC-USZ62-67216

In 1943, Eleanor conducted a tour of inspection in the South Pacific. This photograph was taken in New Caledonia with General Millard Harmon and Admiral William Halsey Jr. on September 15. That evening, Admiral Halsey told Eleanor that she would be allowed to travel to Guadalcanal despite its proximity to the front line. FDR LIBRARY

Could she take a message home for him? I marveled at her hardihood, both physical and mental, she walked for miles, and she saw patients who were grievously and gruesomely wounded. But I marveled most at their expressions as she leaned over them. It was a sight I will never forget."

The young woman who had worried about her appearance and doubted her abilities could no longer be seen; she had transformed herself

■ *Portrait of Eleanor Roosevelt, c. 1940. She motivated and inspired many, her inner resolve evident in her words: "You gain strength, courage and confidence by every experience in which you really stop to look fear in the face. You must do the thing which you think you cannot do."*
LC-USZ62-68110

into a woman willing to travel a long, hard road to provide a glimmer of comfort to those in need. She possessed a rare intensity of compassion and caring; always "determined to do as well as I could," she had become a truly unforgettable sight.

THE 1940 DEMOCRATIC NATIONAL CONVENTION

WHEN RUNNING for his unprecedented third term in office in 1940, Franklin chose for his running mate Henry Wallace, who had served as secretary of agriculture in FDR's cabinet since 1933 and had played a key role in shaping New Deal legislation. Not a lifelong Democrat, Wallace was an unpopular choice. Grumblings surfaced that Franklin, after two terms as president, was becoming haughty, a perception reinforced by his refusal to back down from his choice of Wallace as running mate.

At the Democratic National Convention in July 1940, Eleanor took to the stage on their behalf, delivering a unifying speech that urged the audience to "rise above considerations which are narrow and partisan." The stunned delegates responded by rallying behind the FDR-Wallace ticket, a move that ultimately led to Franklin's 1940 reelection. Eleanor recalled, "While I spoke there was complete silence. It was striking after the pandemonium that had existed." Newspaper headlines bragged, "Mrs. Roosevelt Stills the Tumult of 50,000."

This image of Eleanor was strikingly different from that of the woman who, on attending her first Democratic Party convention in 1912, had "understood nothing of what was going on. . . . Finally, I decided my husband would hardly miss my company . . . so I went home." ■

■ *After her speech at the 1940 Democratic National Convention, Eleanor raises a hand in response to a standing ovation. Applauding behind her is Alben W. Barkley, chairman of the Democratic National Committee.* AP/WORLDWIDE

■ *Eleanor earned the nickname "First Lady of the World" for her international humanitarian journeys. Franklin, incapacitated by polio, depended on her reports about social conditions and public opinion, but she continued to travel even after his death, as in this 1952 trip to Pakistan.* LC-USZ62-113313

"THE STORY IS OVER"

ELEANOR'S TENURE as First Lady came to an abrupt end when Franklin Delano Roosevelt died, on April 12, 1945. She told reporters, "The story is over," but her life of political activism was far from finished. In fact, being out of the White House spotlight afforded her certain advantages: "For the first time in my life I can say just what I want . . . it is wonderful to feel free." Harry S. Truman, FDR's successor, quickly appointed Eleanor to the US delegation to the United Nations; she was the

■ *President Harry S. Truman and Eleanor Roosevelt, 1951. These two collaborated and clashed in political arenas for years. Truman appointed Eleanor to the United Nations' US delegation in 1945 and recommended her for the Nobel Peace Prize in 1964.*

■ *Eleanor discusses the United Nations in an address to Democrats in Philadelphia, 1953.* LC-USZ62-107585

first woman to enjoy this privilege. Subsequently elected chair of the UN Commission on Human Rights, she would play a dominant role in the drafting of the Universal Declaration of Human Rights, a document that defined inalienable international human rights and was adopted by the United Nations in 1948. Despite her successes, however, Dwight D. Eisenhower failed to reappoint her to her UN post when he took office in 1953.

An outspoken Democrat, Eleanor heartily backed presidential nominee and friend Adlai Stevenson in both 1952 and 1956. Despite some initial

■ *The United Nations General Assembly Hall, 1954. Exactly nine years after the United Nations was established, Eleanor took the stage to address the delegates in celebration.*
LC-USZ62-133861

reservations, she also supported John F. Kennedy in his endeavor to capture the hearts and votes of the nation in 1960, appearing alongside him in photographs and campaign advertisements. Kennedy later reappointed Eleanor to the UN delegation, offered her an advisory position with the newly formed Peace Corps, and made her chair of the President's Commission on the Status of Women, where she would continue working, as she had since the 1920s, to further equal rights for women.

■ *Eleanor on the campaign trail with Kennedy and his running mate, Lyndon B. Johnson, 1960. Her support was critical to JFK's success.* LC-USZ62-70670

■ *Eleanor speaks on John F. Kennedy's behalf at the "Citizens for Kennedy" headquarters in New York, 1960. Although it took her some time to warm to him, Eleanor would eventually praise his "quick mind." For his part, Kennedy is said to have remarked of the still-spunky seventy-five-year-old Eleanor: "I am smitten by this woman; absolutely smitten."* LC-USZ62-113650

■ *Chicago, 1954: Eleanor and James E. Doyle attend the seventh annual conference of Americans for Democratic Action, an organization formed to ensure the longevity of New Deal politics. Eleanor helped found the organization in 1947.* LC-USZ62-122607

Eleanor continued to inspire criticism. Her controversial views earned her one of the largest FBI files in history and attracted the vehement attention of many public figures. One of these, Cardinal Francis Spellman, sparred with Eleanor in 1949 over whether federal funding should be provided to religious schools, a dispute that escalated into a personal attack on her. Such attacks, however, never quelled her resolve. She responded to

■ *In 1950, the National Society for Crippled Children honored Eleanor with its Distinguished Service Medal for her diligent work on behalf of children and the handicapped.*
LC-USZ62-108204

Spellman's assessments by writing that "the worthiness of all human beings is in the hands of God." She delivered speeches and kept writing, condemning oppression wherever she saw it, refusing to falter. She staunchly argued against McCarthyism when it gripped the nation in the 1950s, challenged US public policies with which she disagreed, and recommended the creation of and support for the fledgling state of Israel.

■ *Eleanor with Gyalo Thondup, brother of Tibet's Fourteenth Dalai Lama, 1959. Thondup appealed to the United States for aid after attacks on Tibet by Communist China.*
LC-USZ62-114476

■ *Eleanor, her son Elliott, and two of her grandchildren are greeted by sons Franklin Jr. and James (shaking Elliott's hand) as they return from Norway, 1950. Both Franklin Jr. and James followed in their father's political footsteps; they were congressmen when this photograph was taken.* LC-USZ62-128048

■ *Eleanor is awarded the first Mary McLeod Bethune Human Rights Award by the National Council of Negro Women, November 12, 1960. Presenting the prize is the organization's president, Dorothy Height.* LC-USZC2-5811

After her White House years, Eleanor continued her international travels, visiting Lebanon, Israel, India, Pakistan, Japan, and even the Soviet Union to promote humanitarian goals and bring a message of compassion and hope. She also continued her civil rights work, chairing inquiries in Washington, DC, in 1962 on the status of US civil rights activities.

■ *Eleanor addresses the United States Senate, 1955. Once terrified of public speaking, she grew into an accomplished and compelling orator, even becoming the first president's wife to testify before a congressional committee.* LC-USZ62-916918

Eleanor ensured that her opinions were widely heard, and the nation seemed to love it. The woman once denied the privilege of college was ultimately awarded thirty-five honorary degrees. Her popularity in public opinion polls was higher later in her life than it had been when she was First Lady, and it only continued to grow, earning her the Gallup Poll's title of Most Admired Woman—an honor she held long after her death, on November 6, 1962.

DRIVING OUT DISCRIMINATION

■ *Eleanor was deeply devoted to the National Association for the Advancement of Colored People and its goal of civil rights for much of her life. Her involvement only increased as she grew older: she joined the NAACP's board of directors in 1945 and drew attention to the cause of racial justice in her "My Day" column. Here, she is pictured (left) at an NAACP event in the 1950s, flanked by civil rights activists Ruby Hurley and Walter White, and (above) at the NAACP's office with Roy Wilkins, the organization's director during the height of the United States' civil rights movement.* LC-USZ62-77167

BORN INTO A DISTRESSED FAMILY and troubled times, Eleanor Roosevelt could have chosen to passively accept the world as it was and quietly adopt the traditional role of a woman in her society. Instead, she confronted her fears and created the life she wanted to lead: a life of usefulness. She not only dared to imagine a more fulfilling world—one that afforded opportunities for everyone, regardless of sex or color or age—but also devoted herself to making the world she envisioned a reality. Throughout her life, Eleanor offered help to any who wanted it, encouraged those she met who also had a cause, and touched the lives of as many as possible. "There is so much to do, so many engrossing challenges, so many heartbreaking and pressing needs, so much in every day that is profoundly interesting," she declared. She was unique in that she chose to embrace each of those days, her enthusiasm for greater possibilities apparent in all her efforts. ■

■ *Eleanor at UN headquarters, 1947. Her diligent humanitarian work earned her the first United Nations Prize in the Field of Human Rights, awarded posthumously in 1968.* FDR LIBRARY

■ *At her Val-Kill home in New York in 1954, Eleanor reads to a group of students from the Wiltwyck School for Boys.* FDR LIBRARY

■ *Eleanor, c. 1957. A few years later, reminiscing about her life, she would remark, "I could not, at any age, be content to take my place in a corner by the fireside and simply look on."* FDR LIBRARY

SELECTED READING AND SOURCES

Beasley, Maurine H., Holly C. Shulman, and Henry R. Beasley, eds. *The Eleanor Roosevelt Encyclopedia*. Westport, CT: Greenwood Press, 2001.

Black, Allida M., ed. *Courage in a Dangerous World: The Political Writings of Eleanor Roosevelt*. New York: Columbia University Press, 1999.

———. *What I Hope to Leave Behind: The Essential Essays of Eleanor Roosevelt*. Brooklyn, NY: Carlson, 1995.

Caroli, Betty Boyd. *First Ladies*. New York: Oxford University Press, 1987.

Chadakoff, Rochelle, ed. *Eleanor Roosevelt's My Day,* vol. 1. New York: Pharos Books, 1989.

Cook, Blanche Wiesen. *Eleanor Roosevelt*. 2 vols. New York: Viking, 1992–1999.

Emblidge, David, ed. *Eleanor Roosevelt's My Day,* vols. 2, 3. New York: Pharos Books, 1990, 1991.

Goodwin, Doris Kearns. *No Ordinary Time*. New York: Simon & Schuster, 1994.

Lash, Joseph P. *Eleanor: The Years Alone*. New York: Norton, 1972.

———. *Eleanor and Franklin*. Franklin Center, PA: Franklin Library, 1981.

———. *"Life Was Meant to Be Lived": A Centenary Portrait of Eleanor Roosevelt*. New York: Norton, 1984.

———. *Love, Eleanor: Eleanor Roosevelt and Her Friends*. Garden City, NY: Doubleday, 1982.

Roosevelt, Eleanor. *The Autobiography of Eleanor Roosevelt*. New York: Da Capo Press, 1992.

Sicherman, Barbara, and Carol Hurd Green, eds. *Notable American Women: The Modern Period: A Biographical Dictionary*. Cambridge, MA: Belknap Press of Harvard University Press, 1980.

An excellent resource for information and images related to Eleanor and Franklin D. Roosevelt is the FDR Library's website: www.fdrlibrary.marist.edu.

Eleanor is the only First Lady to have had a National Historical Site dedicated to her. This informative website is dedicated to Eleanor's Val-Kill home: www.nps.gov/elro.

ACKNOWLEDGMENTS

The author would like to sincerely thank her editor, Amy Pastan, for all her hard work and diligence. Many thanks to Mark Renovitch at the FDR Library for his help in obtaining several of the photographs in this book. Also, thanks to the teams at the Library of Congress' Publishing Office and at Pomegranate for their support. And—Lynne and Bruce—I am sure my first discovery of Eleanor came from you.

IMAGES

Reproduction numbers, when available, are given for all items in the collections of the Library of Congress. Unless otherwise noted, Library of Congress images are from the Prints and Photographs Division. To order reproductions, note the LC- number provided with the image; where no number exists, note the Library division and the title of the item. Direct your request to:

The Library of Congress
Photoduplication Service
Washington DC 20540-4570
(202) 707-5640; www.loc.gov